Country Stars Shine

INSIGHTS TO YOUR FAVORITE COUNTRY ARTISTS...
Their Lives, Loves and Reflections

Compiled by

LISA MURR CHAPMAN

Eggman Publishing Company, Inc.

Country Stars Shine

Copyright ©1995 by Lisa Murr Chapman

All rights reserved. Written authorization is required from the
publisher to use or reproduce any part of this book. Brief quotations in
published critical reviews or articles are permitted without
written authorization.

Design by Dianna Meadows, DesignWorks

ISBN: 1-886371-03-2

Country Stars Shine

This collection is enthusiastically dedicated to each and every country music fan:

"If I didn't have fans,
what would I have?"

–George Strait

———————— *Country Stars Shine* ————————

"All the disappointments we've gone through will turn out in a positive way."

— *Deborah Allen*

Country Stars Shine

"Being successful in business doesn't mean success in life."

— *John Anderson*

Country Stars Shine

"The isolation, the poverty, that's where I came from. That's what makes you fight."

– *Chet Atkins*

Country Stars Shine

"To meet people I idolize: Ernest Tubb, Count Basie, Willie Nelson, Merle Haggard...has been more than enough reward for me."

— *Ray Benson*
Asleep at the Wheel

Country Stars Shine

"To get a painful point across in a beautiful way, it doesn't seem to hurt so bad."

— Matraca Berg
on her songs

Country Stars Shine

"We all have problems; you have to take them as they come and deal with 'em the best way you can."

— *Clint Black*

Country Stars Shine

"…touch on the emotions so that it relieves the pain."

— *Suzy Bogguss*

Country Stars Shine

"We all had parents who tried to bring us up the right way."

—*Joe Bonsall*
The Oak Ridge Boys

Country Stars Shine

"You gotta be thankful for what you got and treat people like you want to be treated."

— *Garth Brooks*

Country Stars Shine

"He let us know that he loved us a lot. That's what I try to do for my kids."

— *Kix Brooks, Brooks & Dunn on his father*

Country Stars Shine

"I know what it's like not to have anything and I appreciate what I have right now."

— *Marty Brown*

Country Stars Shine

"All that stuff ain't gonna get you
to heaven and that's where
I want to wind up."

— *T. Graham Brown*

Country Stars Shine

"Having a baby is a big-time growing process, emotionally and spiritually."

— *Paulette Carlson*

Country Stars Shine

"To be growing up and out
is what it's all about."

— Mary Chapin Carpenter

Country Stars Shine

"Everything comes back the way it should if you try hard to be real upright."

— *Carlene Carter*

Country Stars Shine

"I think we're living in a time
when people are so scared
to open themselves up."

— *Lionel Cartwright*

Country Stars Shine

"Being inducted into the Country Music Hall of Fame was the greatest honor of my career."

— Johnny Cash

Country Stars Shine

"On the surface of life everything can look placid and normal, but unseen there's this whole life evolving."

— *Rosanne Cash*

Country Stars Shine

"It's tough out there for women."

— Cee Cee Chapman

Country Stars Shine

"My Mother's the only one left now and I take care of her."

— *Mark Chesnutt*

Country Stars Shine

"It's a healthy thing to express what you feel."

— *Mark Collie*

Country Stars Shine

"Nobody needs help to get through the good times, and the bad times will always get better with the help of God."

— *John Conlee*

Country Stars Shine

"I adore my wife. Every year and every day, I love her even more."

— *Jerry Clower*

Country Stars Shine

"The first time I ever heard music I was hooked."

— *Rodney Crowell*

Country Stars Shine

"I feel I owe God a big favor."

— *Billy Ray Cyrus*

Country Stars Shine

"I have huge respect for the working man."

— *Charlie Daniels*

Country Stars Shine

"If it's not the Lord's will and it's not His time, it's not going to happen."

— Linda Davis

Country Stars Shine

"All couples have their small jealousies and I think a little of that is healthy."

— *Billy Dean*

Country Stars Shine

"It's like they say,
'Blessings come in disguises.'"

– *Joe Diffie*

Country Stars Shine

"I hated my life. So I took refuge in writing."

— John Dittrich, Restless Heart
on his teen years

Country Stars Shine

"I'm one of the biggest country fans that ever lived."

– Holly Dunn

Country Stars Shine

"My sisters are all so low-key. I always tell Mom, 'Think how boring it would've been if I were as nice as them.'"

– Kim Forester
The Forester Sisters

—————————— *Country Stars Shine*——

"...every time you touch the spider
web of life it has repercussions
all over the place..."

— Radney Foster

Country Stars Shine

"We didn't have a dime, but all of us kids went to college."

— Cleve Francis

Country Stars Shine

"I couldn't accomplish all I've done without Him."

—*Janie Fricke*

Country Stars Shine

"I've learned just to accept things the way they are."

— *Steve Gatlin*
The Gatlin Brothers

Country Stars Shine

"When you reach 40, I think something in you wants to slow down a bit and smell the roses."

— Teddy Gentry
Alabama

Country Stars Shine

"My parents wanted me to be independent. I feel very lucky they didn't shelter me."

— *Terry Gibbs*

Country Stars Shine

"You gotta laugh it off
or you'll drive yourself crazy."

— *Vince Gill*

Country Stars Shine

"Nobody knows what feeling good means until they've been to the point where they wonder if they'll ever feel good again."

— *Vern Gosdin*

Country Stars Shine

"I get my britches on like everybody else does."

— *Clinton Gregory*

Country Stars Shine

"There's the guy I'd love to be and the guy I am, and I'm somewhere in between."

— *Merle Haggard*

Country Stars Shine

"I'm proud of Miss Dixie."

— Tom T. Hall
about his wife

Country Stars Shine

"Being a parent is incredibly important to me, but incredibly difficult."

— *Emmylou Harris*

Country Stars Shine

"When I'm home, my family gets 150%."

— *Mark Herndon*
Alabama

Country Stars Shine

"Just because I'm 26 years old doesn't mean I haven't lived."

– Faith Hill

Country Stars Shine

"My Father might be the only truly good man I've ever known."

— Alan Jackson

Country Stars Shine

"Country music can survive
something different.
It survived me!"

— *Waylon Jennings*

Country Stars Shine

"I'm country and I'm proud of it
and I love it and
it's deep inside me."

— George Jones

Country Stars Shine

"When I came to Nashville, I had nothing...no confidence, very little self-esteem."

– Naomi Judd

Country Stars Shine

"I go by gut feelings and what my heart wants to do."

— *Sammy Kershaw*

Country Stars Shine

"There was a time in my life where my perfectionism kinda overrode everything and I missed good times because of that."

— Hal Ketchum

Country Stars Shine

"I've got enough money to buy hairspray, so it's fine!"

— *Alison Krauss*

Country Stars Shine

"I'm just trying to lead a spiritual life."

— *Kris Kristofferson*

Country Stars Shine

"The only way to be happy is to be happy with yourself."

— *Tracy Lawrence*

Country Stars Shine

"Stand up for what you believe in, face things up front and be honest."

— *Chris LeDoux*

Country Stars Shine

"I'm a very private person, a loner."

— *Patty Loveless*

Country Stars Shine

"You've got to jump in head first
and never look back."

— *Loretta Lynn*

Country Stars Shine

"I'm very open and honest about my feelings, if you ask me."

— *Shelby Lynn*

Country Stars Shine

"Country music is about life, and we sing about life as we see it."

— Raul Malo
The Mavericks

Country Stars Shine

"The two things you must give your children are roots and wings."

— *Barbara Mandrell*

Country Stars Shine

"You have to be open to criticism if you're gonna grow."

— Kathy Mattea

Country Stars Shine

"I try to find songs that portray women with dignity and respect."

— Martina McBride

Country Stars Shine

"Things work out for a reason.
You have to believe in it or it'll make
you crazy trying to analyze it."

— *Terry McBride*
McBride & The Ride

Country Stars Shine

"I just go with the flow."

— Bill McCorvey
Pirates of the Mississippi

Country Stars Shine

"I'm kind of a weird father."

— Ronnie McDowell
on his love for fun in his home

Country Stars Shine

"You've got to work at marriage. I don't care if you marry the person of your all-time dreams. It's a lot of work."

—*Reba McEntire*

Country Stars Shine

"I feel like I'm the luckiest guy in the world."

— *Tim McGraw*

Country Stars Shine

"Variety is what makes the world go 'round."

– *Mark Miller*
Sawyer Brown

Country Stars Shine

"We were poor but we never thought of ourselves as poor."

— *Roger Miller*

Country Stars Shine

"I believe my circumstances have given me an inner strength, and I thank God for my many blessings."

— *Ronnie Milsap*

Country Stars Shine

"If I ever left the Opry, I'd have to fire myself!"

—Bill Monroe

Country Stars Shine

"They're not coming out to see me.
I'm coming out to see them."

— John Michael Montgomery
on his fans

———————— *Country Stars Shine*————————

"I've always said that if I ever win any kind of award, my first thanks will be to God, but my second will be to Ralph Emery."

—*Lorrie Morgan*

Country Stars Shine

"I just go through life. I don't really think much about age."

– *Michael Martin Murphey*

Country Stars Shine

"I'd recommend being a father
at any age."

— *Willie Nelson*

Country Stars Shine

"People who write songs get their hearts broken all the time."

— *Robert Ellis Orral*

Country Stars Shine

"My friends have always been a very important part of my life."

— K.T. Oslin

Country Stars Shine

"What's most important to me is
that my kids will hopefully look
back one day and say that
I was a good mom."

— *Marie Osmond*

Country Stars Shine

"You have to get your happiness from inside yourself."

— *Paul Overstreet*

Country Stars Shine

"I don't have to control everything that happens in life."

— Lee Roy Parnell

Country Stars Shine

"Every diet I ever fell off was because of a potato of one kind or another!"

— *Dolly Parton*

Country Stars Shine

"When I get knocked down,
I just get back up."

— Johnny Paycheck

Country Stars Shine

"Don't ever be afraid to tell someone you love them."

— Minnie Pearl

Country Stars Shine

"The Person who planned all this is bigger than all of us."

— Charlie Pride

Country Stars Shine

"If you're going to be somewhere,
you might as well be happy."

— Duane Propes
Little Texas

Country Stars Shine

"I stare at the ceiling for hours!
People think I'm comatose,
but I'm actually composing."

— *Eddie Rabbit*

Country Stars Shine

"We're just like everybody else.
We get aggravated, we
even have words
with each other."

— *Marty Raybon*
Shenandoah

Country Stars Shine

"The most precious, wonderful thing you can do in your life is have a child."

— *Collin Raye*

Country Stars Shine

"I've been more outspoken and I've learned from that. If I don't, it's me who will suffer."

— *Ronna Reeves*

Country Stars Shine

"They say you can't go home,
so the trick is never to leave."

— Harold Reid
The Statlers

Country Stars Shine

"We would like to believe that human beings are capable of loving each other forever."

— *Mike Reid*

Country Stars Shine

"It's real hard for me to write a cheating song when it's not something I bank on."

— *Marty Roe*
Diamond Rio

Country Stars Shine

"It's fun for me to compete as long as I know the rules."

— *Kenny Rogers*

Country Stars Shine

"I just like to enjoy my family and live as long as I possibly can."

— *Roy Rogers*

Country Stars Shine

"Being happy with yourself, having good health, and doing what you wanna do."

— *Billy Joe Royal*
on his definition of success

Country Stars Shine

"I didn't have any sense when I was drinking. I finally just said, 'I don't want to ruin my life.'"

— *Ricky Van Shelton*

Country Stars Shine

"If you're satisfied with what you're doing, that's all you're ever gonna do."

— *Danny Shirley*
Confederate Railroad

Country Stars Shine

"The family is where God's heart is."

— *Ricky Skaggs*

—————————— *Country Stars Shine* ——————————

"When you get older, you're
thankful for the way you
were raised."

— *Richard Sterbin*
The Oak Ridge Boys

Country Stars Shine

"I learned a lot about independence from him."

— *Lisa Stewart*
on her Dad

Country Stars Shine

"It was like ripping my heart out and stomping on it for a couple of years."

— *Doug Stone on his divorce*

Country Stars Shine

"My motto is,
'When in doubt, go see Momma.'"

– Marty Stuart

Country Stars Shine

"If you take everything seriously, you'll get your heart broken."

— *Jack Sundrud*
Great Plains

Country Stars Shine

"Time gets more and more precious the older you get."

— *Pam Tillis*

Country Stars Shine

"I've learned a little more patience for the minor things."

— Aaron Tippin

Country Stars Shine

"I try to live a Christian way."

— *Randy Travis*

Country Stars Shine

"I just try to take everything one day at a time."

— *Travis Tritt*

Country Stars Shine

"I have a lot of respect for those gals out there that are single moms and have to go to work and leave their children."

— *Tanya Tucker*

Country Stars Shine

"I thought I was taking up somebody's spot who worked harder for it than I had."

— *Conway Twitty*
on his early success

Country Stars Shine

"That's what life is all about: giving back."

— Steve Wariner

Country Stars Shine

"A lot of times people don't change until they have to."

— *Kevin Welch*

Country Stars Shine

"I'm a truly helpless romantic just trying to survive in the '90s!"

— *Lari White*

Country Stars Shine

"I don't think success should be equated to how many dollars you make."

— *Don Williams*

Country Stars Shine

"On weekends friends would come over and we'd have hootenannies. I just thought everybody's family did that."

— *Joy White*

Country Stars Shine

"It's been good for me to have seen a lot of changes."

— *Hank Williams, Jr.*

Country Stars Shine

"Sometimes shyness can be mistaken for weakness."

—*Kelly Willis*

Country Stars Shine

"It's a comfort to know that someone else feels like you feel when you're all torn down by heartache."

— *Curtis Wright*

Country Stars Shine

"You have to keep believing
in yourself."

— *Michelle Wright*

Country Stars Shine

"...communicate with people. That's the key to success."

– *Tammy Wynette*

Country Stars Shine

"Life is so weird.
Why try to figure it out?"

— *Wynonna*

Country Stars Shine

Women cheat and they drink, too –
so why not sing about it?

— *Trisha Yearwood*

Country Stars Shine

"The only thing certain is uncertainty."

— Dwight Yoakam

ORDER FORM

CHECK ANY OF THE FOLLOWING:

____ Please send information on the rest of the books in this series.

____ Please send *Country Stars Shine* @ $5.95 each: Qty: _____ $ _____

Name _____

Street address _____

_____

City, St, Zip _____

Daytime phone ( ) _____

Gift Message _____

_____

_____

Additional gift information may be listed on the back of this form.

Merchandise Total	$ _____
Shipping & Handling add $1ea.	
Subtotal	$ _____
TN residents add 8.25% sales tax	_____
TOTAL	$ _____

METHOD OF PAYMENT:

____ Check or money order payable to Eggman is enclosed.

____ Charge to my: __ VISA __ MasterCard
__ Discover

Card# _____ Exp. ____

Signature required for credit card purchases:

_____

Enclose payment and order form and mail to:
Eggman Publishing, Inc.
2909 Poston Avenue   Suite 203
Nashville, TN 37203

THANK YOU! Your order will be shipped within 1-3 weeks.

OR CALL 1-800-409-7277